Water Signs

Ayushi Sanjay Acharya

BookLeaf Publishing
India | USA | UK

Dedication

for the dreamers, the feelers, the ones who carry oceans
within—

Preface

may these words reflect the depths you hold and the
waves you create

Acknowledgements

for all the moments, places and people that inspired
these words, thank you.

1. pretty grief

you swallow me whole just to spit me out
you wrap your arms around my throat and rock me like
a child
you give me so much comfort and you hate me so much
you come to me uninvited and overstay your welcome
you whisper to me gently, 'I'll never go away'
you are a nightmare wrapped in gleaming crystals
I beg you to stay
I can't breathe when you're around me
you give me so much meaning

3. desert nights

I tell you about the dream I had
the one about when the world ends but we decide to stay

you laugh and hold out your hand
when I go to grab it you disappear

your voice surrounds me, "stop taking life too seriously"

but how will I survive without you when the world ends
and I decide to stay

you trick me, you play games
you know I'll never win

you fill a void but you never wanted to do that
you remind me that the world was ending and that you
never were going to stay

And here I am right where you left me

now I starve in the desert
the stars dancing for me,
teasing me
"how did you end up all alone?" they want to know

how do I tell them that this is where you left me
this is where you told me to wait for you

how do I tell the stars that the only places you lead me
are
lonely, vast, empty, and filled with nothingness

4. sienna

when your color feels ugly
define ugly
your skin is the color of the soil, iced coffee, pennies,
almonds
peanut butter, potatoes, cinnamon
toffee

your color is the same color of your grandmother's arms
as she walked to school

your color is the same color of your mother's eyes when
she saw you for the first time

your brown is just the sun's love trapped in your flesh

5. the operation

you said it's time to lay down
you said you'll do everything
you can to make me safe
your breath is above me, it revives me

my last thought before the darkness "how did I live so
long without this?"

did you want to fix me from the start?

how do you slice me open to make me whole again

6.

7. lonely but make it cute

it's all the memories we share that you do not know / the memories I have of us that happened when you weren't looking / the empty hotel rooms / me convincing people who love me that you love me / the unanswered text messages / the weeks of silence / the months of silence / while you were gone I was making memories of us / putting my car in park to meet the girls for dinner / willing myself to get out / putting on a smile with sad eyes / they know I am so sad / all my words are about you / getting so drunk / am I always so drunk / telling the girl in the bathroom about you / trying that dress on in case you call / does depression feel like drowning / I'm walking through all our past, current & future memories / you're no where to be found / you're constantly there / your presence fills me / completes me / sometimes I don't even notice I'm all alone

8. scorpio

even in your shadows there is solace
you take me blindfolded through these parts
never been in a place as dark as you

you pull me into the storm
with a single glance,
a magnet of fire and ice,
all at once.
an abyss I can't resist
even when I know how deep it goes

your attention are really just flames I am drowning in
that doesn't ask for forgiveness,
that doesn't need to be understood—
and still,
I find myself falling,
knowing I may never rise again

how can I learn all your secrets
why can I touch you but I cannot know you
you are getting weary of all the questions

you need so little and I want to devour you whole
you only respond to my obsession with possession
being yours for moments will never be enough
passion cannot build the bones of our home

9. pisces

when you go to heaven
we'll tell them you don't have a heart
because you left the pieces in so many places over the
years

you move like water
flowing in currents you can't quite name—
a ripple in the quiet,
a storm in the stillness.
your reflection is all sky and the sea
and dreams
that stretch beyond the horizon.

you speak in whispers,
but there is a truth in the silence,
a knowing that rests beneath the surface.

The world feels both close and distant

when you're near,

this heart you left is a place where the tides rise and fall,
where love is both a current and a shore.

you give so much without asking,
a river that never runs dry,
yet the depths of you remain hidden,
like the secrets of the ocean floor.

a mystery in human form,
forever swimming between the stars and the waves,
always searching,
always lost,
but somehow, you always feel like home.

10. highlights shouldn't feel this low

The light we chase
is always just ahead,
flickering like a promise
too far to touch.

We wait for the warmth
to fill the empty spaces,
but instead, we feel
the weight of shadows
creeping in.

We were told
the brightest moments would elevate us,
yet here we are,
standing beneath them,
hollow,
looking up,
feeling the distance
grow with every breath.

The highlights should be high—
a lift,
a spark,
a fire
that turns the dark to something more
than just a place to wait.

But in the silence,
in the waiting,
they feel distant,
almost like ghosts
fading before we even reach them.

The highlights shouldn't feel this low.
They should lift us,
but here we are,
held by the gravity of something
we can't quite grasp.

11. you missed the best part

You missed the days I stood tall,
when my laughter filled the room
and I was whole,
before the world bent me into something different.

You weren't there for the victories,
the moments when I shone alone,
when I didn't need anyone
to validate what I had found in myself.

You missed the quiet joy,
the nights I learned how to dance
without your shadow trailing behind,
the peace I built in the spaces you once filled.

You missed the spark,
the fire I kindled in my own chest,
burning brighter without you,
not because of you.

But I remember how you came
when the dust settled,
when I was softer,
a little broken,
but somehow still beautiful in the cracks.

You reached for the pieces you never valued,
the parts of me that had healed
without your hands.

And now, you long for what you never earned—
the best parts of my life,
the ones you'll never have
because you left before you could see
how much I was capable of becoming
without you.

12. cancer

She is the moon in human form,
quiet and constant,
her tides rising and falling with the pull of unseen
forces.
Her heart is a shell,
strong and protective,
but soft beneath the surface,
a safe haven for those who find their way in.

She loves with the depth of the ocean,
gentle and fierce,
nurturing what she touches
until it blooms or fades in her care.

Her emotions, like waves,
crash and retreat,
but her love is steady—
a rhythm that always returns.

Her home is her sanctuary,

where she builds worlds from comfort and warmth,
a place where you are always welcomed
with open arms and a quiet understanding.
She listens without judgment,
feels without fear,
and when she loves,
it is with everything she has.

But beware the storm she hides within,
for when she is hurt,
the tides can rise,
flooding everything in their path.
Yet, even in her anger,
there is tenderness—
the storm always passes,
and she will rebuild,
stronger, softer,
like the moon that guides the night.

13. our champagne season

paint the pretty picture
the jewels around my neck are blinding
the sari wrapped tight around my waist, my chest is
suffocating
my bangles make this damn sound every time you grab
my hand
the alcohol isn't doing its job because I don't forgive you
yet
it's champagne season baby
and this time we have permission to let go of our
inhibitions
this time we get to pretend we are thankful we found
this love in hopelessness
this time you can mask that you are in love with
someone else
this time I can hide that we haven't slept in the same bed
in months
this time we get to promise each other we will always be
together
you're drinking straight from the bottle

If I lick the champagne from your lips, will I drown in it
too?
the champagne covers the lies we tell each other in the
daylight
the champagne helps us hold each other in the
moonlight
it's always champagne season for us baby
the champagne protects us
prevents the thoughts of the devastation
the calamity
that is me and you

14. museum of her

She's a gallery,
a room full of moments—
each one, a painting,
each one, a scar.
The walls hold the weight
of what she's seen,
what she's been
and what she's lost
in the space between the years.

There are portraits of the little girl
who believed in forever,
her eyes wide with dreams
and a heart full of firsts.
Her laughter echoed in halls
that now feel hollow,
fading at the edges,
like sunlight turning to dusk.

There are rooms marked *Before*

where she wore tenderness like a cloak,
where she let herself be soft,
before the world taught her
to steel herself.
Before the heartache came
and she learned to hold the pieces
instead of the whole.

Then came the room of questions—
Why does she feel too much?
Why does she have to be strong?
Why do the parts of her
that used to bloom
now wilt in the quiet?
She stands in the middle of it,
trying to find the girl she was
amidst the dust and the change.

there's a room marked *Now*,
a space she's still filling,
a space where the cracks
have started to shine,
where the edges of her past
don't define her
but remind her
of how far she's come.
How many lives she's lived

in the years between the before and the after.

She walks through each room
with her hands held high—
no longer afraid of the weight,
no longer hiding
behind the frames
of the woman she was supposed to be.
Her heart is a work in progress,
and she is learning
to see herself
as the masterpiece.

15. heartaches are only for hotel rooms

heartaches are only for hotel rooms,
where the bed feels too wide and the silence is loud
the walls don't know your name
they echo with every thought
you can't stop having.
the city hums outside,
but inside, the hours drag their feet
across the floor,
heavy with what was once easy
and now is just a ghost
in a room with no past.

I trace the space between us,
thinking of the words we left unspoken,
words that slip like water
through the cracks of the night.
the room smells faintly of something
that used to be sweet—

maybe the Merlot,
maybe a dream.

heartaches are only for hotel rooms,
where nothing is yours
but the ache in your chest,
the way your hands don't know
what to do with the emptiness.
they curl around the pillow,
searching for something
to hold that won't slip away.

I used to think love
was something that filled rooms—
but love,
like the best things,
can vanish without warning,
leaving you alone
with the things you wish
you hadn't said.
with the things you wish
you could forget.

heartaches are only for hotel rooms,
where you close the door on what remains,
and try to sleep,
but the bed,

the silence,
and the miles between us
are all the things you'll never leave behind.

16. happy for you

I saw your name today,
threaded into a conversation
that had nothing to do with me.

It hung there, weightless,
but still managed to press
against the quietest parts of my memory.

I heard you're doing well—
a new city, a new love,
a life stretching like a sunrise
I'm not awake to see.

They say time heals,
but they don't tell you how it scars too.
How the ache dulls but never really leaves,
how you can move forward
but still look back
when no one's watching.

I want you to be happy.
I want that to be enough for me.
And maybe someday it will be,
when the corners of my heart
stop clinging to the shadows of your touch.

For now, I'll practice—
clapping softly from a distance,
cheering for a life
I am no longer part of.
Happy for you.
Almost meant it.

Let me try again
I'm happy for you,
even when the words
stick in my throat
and the ache of what we were
finds its way back
in the spaces between
"happy" and "for you."

17. waves

Time bends like waves, unbound, untrue,
Stretching in swells, retreating from view.

An hour can crash with the weight of the sea,
Or drift like foam, slipping quietly free.

Each crest a promise, each trough a sigh,
Moments rising, then fading, a whisper goodbye.

What once felt eternal, now ebbs away,
The tide erasing the footprints of day.

The shoreline shifts with the passing of years,
Washed clean by joy, reshaped by tears.

But the waves keep coming, steady and strong,
A rhythm that hums where we all belong.

And so, we float in their ceaseless embrace,

Carried forward by currents we cannot trace.

For time is a wave, and we are its song,
Forever fleeting, yet endlessly long.

18. drowning for the plot

She waits at the edge of the story,
where the tide laps at her toes,
her heart an anchor
dragging against the pull of what-ifs.

Every wave brings a fragment of him:
a glance, a half-formed promise,
the memory of his voice
threading through her silence.

She rewrites the chapters in her head,
how he might turn back,
how his shadow might stretch long enough
to meet her in the sun.

But he never turns,
and the sun sets just the same.
The ocean rises, slow and sure,
seeping into the cracks of her resolve.

She doesn't move ---
the saltwater feels like love if you stay long enough.

This is how she sinks,
not with thrashing, but with hope,
holding her breath for a scene
that will never be written.

19. don't forget to water me

You are cracked clay,
a pot that leaks where the light should live.
Still, I fill you,
pouring care into the places
others said weren't worth saving.
Your edges cut me sometimes—
sharp with your past,
jagged with the weight of mistakes
you won't let go.

But I trace them anyway,
my hands learning the map of you.
I don't ask for perfection,
only the effort to grow.
To take root in this love,
to meet me in the soil we share.

But even flowers need watering,
and I wonder if you remember
I'm wilting too.

You're flawed,
but so am I,
and still I stand in the garden
we built from fractured things.

Hoping you'll learn
that even broken pots
can hold enough.

I see your cracks,
the places where the light escapes
and the shadows pool.
Your edges are uneven,
your roots tangled in storms
you never asked for.

But I stay,
hands dirty with the soil of your growth,
nurturing the parts you hide
in the corners of your heart.

You bloom in fragments,
petals opening slow,
a beauty only visible up close.
I love you in the droughts,
when your words fall sharp and dry,
and in the floods,

when your sorrow spills over the brim.

Even when your branches twist
away from the sun,
I wait in the shade,
believing in the green beneath.

But love is a two-way garden,
and I am parched.

Don't forget to water me—
I too am alive,
roots deep in the same soil,
reaching for the same sky.

20. forecast says rain all year

I saw it coming—
the heavy sky, the cold wind's warning.
Still, I stood without an umbrella,
arms open, waiting for the storm.
You were the rain I wished for,
soft at first,
gentle enough to make me believe
I could bloom in your downpour.

But love like yours falls unevenly,
dripping from the eaves
while I stand soaked to the skin.

Every drop whispers your name,
but you don't hear mine in the thunder.

I've learned the pattern now:
how clouds gather over your silences,
how the ache pools in the low places.

Still, I can't stop looking up,
hoping you'll spill light instead of shadow.

The forecast doesn't change.
It's rain all year,
a steady fall of what could never be.
And I, stubborn and yearning,
remain in the storm.

21. to our daughters

my mother carried me across borders I never saw, the
ground beneath us shifted with every step
new soil, unfamiliar skies
a world that she did not know the rules but pretended to,
for my sake.
I carried the weight of my new two worlds
on my shoulders so you could walk free of it.

the old one, heavy with stories,
scented with cardamom, regrets and rain,
stitched with the threads of a history
you may never fully understand.

and the new one, sprawling,
unfamiliar, sharp-edged—
I drove recklessly, exposed and vigilant
I bled so you wouldn't have to.

my mother worked with hands that never rested,

sacrificing softness for survival.
I know now that it was all for you.
every hour, every breath
was a prayer for the life you would live.

I silenced the songs of my mother tongue,
so your voice could rise above accents
that might have chained you to invisibility.

I see you now, speaking new languages
the women before you could never master,
dreaming dreams
these women dared not imagine.

the world I built for you is a mosaic:
a patchwork of what I carried,
what I learned,
and what I let go of.

the part I held onto is yours:
the resilience of women
who loved in whispers,
the fire of ancestors
who carved out a place in the impossible.

I will give you what my mother gave to me
a chance to dream of a life

that is entirely your own.
It is a gift I do not regret.
Even if you never know
what it cost me.
I will never know what is cost my mother and her
mother and her mother and her mother.

22. cherry red rage

Grief wears red in my heart—
not the soft blush of mourning,
but the sharp, biting hue of anger.

It flares like fire under my ribs,
a heat I cannot swallow,
burning through memories too tender to touch.
I rage because love had no warning,
because time took what it should have left.

I rage at the silence,
the hollow where your voice once lived,
at the cruelty of a world
that spins without you.

And yet, from this fury,
something blooms.
A fierce beauty rises in the ashes,
petals of cherry red unfolding,
as if my anger has learned to create

what it could not save.

The fire in me plants seeds
where despair once grew.

This rage—it doesn't destroy;
it colors the sky,
paints my grief in shades of survival.

Cherry red becomes a banner,
a testament to the love that burned so brightly
it could not fade without a fight.

Grief is a fire that burns in jagged lines,
a cherry red rage that stains the skin,
sharp and sudden,
like a storm that doesn't warn you
before it tears the air apart.

It rises in the chest,
hot and suffocating,
cracking bones with its weight.
There are no gentle edges,
only the harshness of wanting
what you can never have again.

But anger, in its rawness,

has a beauty of its own—
a wildness that tears apart the old
to make room for something new.

Like the first blossom after a winter storm,
it blooms in defiance,
bold and unforgiving.

It screams in the quietest places,
in the places you thought you had forgotten.

It shatters the calm of what was,
and leaves you with something jagged—
something real.

And when the fire burns out,
and the ash settles,
you are left standing,
still scorched,
but with a heart that has learned
how to grow in the cracks.

23. made me think of you

the rain today fell softly,
like the way your reassuring words used to trace
the edges of my uncertainty.

each drop carried a memory—
a laugh, a fight,
a silence we couldn't fill.

the song on the radio stopped me.
because it was ours—
when we were girls together
it sounded like the late night bars
where you guided me through the boys and the lights
to the dance floor

I still associate vodka tonics with beginnings,
when the world between us was small enough
to hold in our hands.

we were girls together

"can you tell my mom I was with you last night?"
"is he cheating on me?"
"can I post this picture?"
"will it always hurt this much?"

for a moment, I wanted to call you,
but time has frayed the lines between us

forever feels so fragile now,
a word too big
for hands that couldn't hold it.

maybe some friendships are meant to live
only in the chapters they belong to
but no feeling quite can replace
being girls together